# Sleeping Beauty

Original story by Charles Perrault

Retold by Pippa Goodhart

Series Advisor Professor Kimberley Reynolds

Illustrated by Bee Willey

**OXFORD**
UNIVERSITY PRESS

# Letter from the Author

Once, when I was about your age, somebody in my class at school had a birthday party. Just about everybody was invited ... except me! I minded very, very much being left out like that. So I feel sorry for the left-out fairy in this story, even though she is nasty!

I don't live in a palace and have fairies visiting. But I do live in a lovely house that my husband designed and built. We have a pond in the garden. On summer evenings there are sometimes dragonflies with beautiful wings flying around the pond. They look a little like fairies.

*Pippa Goodhart*

Once upon a time, a king and queen wanted a child. When the Queen gave birth to a baby girl, they were proud and happy.

'We must give her a truly lovely name,' said the Queen.

'And we must have a grand party,' said the King. 'Everyone will want to come and see her.'

They thought of lots of names for their baby. At last they found just the right one.

'She was born at dawn,' said the Queen. 'So we should call her Aurora. Aurora means "the dawn".'

'Perfect!' said the King. 'And her party shall be perfect too.'

The King wrote invitations to lots of people.

'I will invite the fairies, because fairies can give our daughter the best gifts of all,' he said. The King found the names of seven fairies. 'Seven is a lucky number, so that's good,' said the King.

The party was lit with lanterns, and there was music from trumpets and drums. Everyone was dressed in wonderful clothes. There was a feast of food served on gold plates, and the seven fairies ate using diamond-studded knives and forks.

Princess Aurora lay in her cradle. All the guests were happy and laughing and eating.

'Oh, this is perfect!' said the King.

'Just perfect,' said the Queen.

But just then ...

# Crash!

The door opened. Wind swirled into the room. There, on the doorstep, stood a nasty-looking fairy.

The music and laughter stopped.

'Why was I not invited to this party?' said the nasty fairy.

'Oh dear. You should have been!' said the King, hurrying to bring the fairy into the party. 'I am so sorry, Madam Fairy. I didn't know about you, so I couldn't invite you. But I invite you now. Do sit down.'

The King himself laid a new place at the table for the nasty fairy. But he didn't have more knives and forks with diamonds in. She was given plain gold ones.

'So I am not as welcome as those other fairies?' said the nasty fairy.

'Oh dear, oh dear,' said the Queen.

The fairies began to give their gifts. One by one they came forward.

'My gift will give you beauty,' said the first fairy, waving her wand over baby Aurora.

'My gift will make you clever,' said the second fairy.

The next four fairies gave Aurora gifts to make her kind and caring, and to make her good at dancing and singing. But then ...

# BANG!

That nasty fairy hit the floor with her stick.

'You've forgotten me again!' she said. She pointed at baby Aurora. 'My gift to you is that one day you will prick your finger on a spindle, and you will die!'

'No!' said the Queen.

'Now you see why you should have invited me!' said the nasty fairy.

But there was still the youngest fairy who hadn't yet given her gift.

'I don't have the power to undo that bad spell,' she said. 'But my gift is to make Aurora sleep for a hundred years rather than die.'

Well, that was the end of the party.

The King ordered every spindle in the kingdom to be burned. He got a nanny to keep a close watch on Princess Aurora. He made very sure that she was safe as she grew up. For sixteen years all went well.

But when Aurora was no longer a child, her nanny left. There came a day when the King and Queen were out for a visit, and Princess Aurora thought, *Now I'm going to explore the whole palace!*

Aurora climbed up a turret where she had never been before. At the top she found a room with an old lady in it. This old lady had never heard of the King's rule about spindles.

'What are you doing?' asked Aurora.

'I am spinning thread,' said the old lady, giving her spindle a twist.

'Please may I have a go?' asked Aurora.
Of course Aurora had never seen anybody
spinning before. She reached out a finger ...
and pricked it on the spindle spike.

Straight away, Aurora fell fast asleep onto the floor. The old lady couldn't wake Aurora, so she called for help.

When the King and Queen came home, they were very upset.

'We shouldn't have left her alone,' they said. They got a doctor to try and wake Aurora. They tried slapping her hands. They put cold water on her face.

Nothing woke her. 'I think we must send for that kind young fairy again,' said the Queen. 'She will help us.'

The kind fairy came, and she told them, 'Aurora will sleep for a hundred years. But it will be so sad for her to wake up after all that time, and find that you have died. So shall I make you all sleep too?'

'Oh, yes,' said the King and Queen. 'We want to be here when she wakes.'

The kind fairy touched the King and the Queen with her wand. 'Sleep now for as long as Aurora sleeps,' she said. She touched her wand to all the servants and animals too. Everything living in the palace slept, even the fires and fountains.

The kind fairy promised Aurora, 'A prince will wake you from your sleep when the time is right.'

As the kind fairy left the palace, she touched her wand to a tree outside. A great thick forest of trees and thorns grew around the palace to keep Princess Aurora safe.

For a hundred years everything in that palace slept. Outside, the world went on as usual. From time to time somebody would ask, 'What is behind that big hedge of thorns?'

At first people knew the answer.

'A princess sleeps there, along with the King and Queen and everyone else. After a hundred years they will all wake up.'

Some people thought, *I will go and rescue them!* But everyone who tried to hack through the hedge found that they could not. Those magic thorns were strong.

As time passed, the stories changed.

'There's something behind the hedge. See those turrets? It must be a castle. I think an ogre lives there. Or ghosts.'

But one day a young prince called Florimond came riding into the forest. He didn't believe the stories about an ogre or ghosts.

At last he found an old woodcutter who told him, 'Well there is another story. My grandfather told it to me. He said that there is a beautiful princess asleep, and only a kiss from a prince can wake her.'

'Well I am a prince!' said Prince Florimond.

So Prince Florimond pulled out his sword and he hacked at the trees. This time the trees magically opened up a path in front of him. Florimond walked into the palace full of sleepers.

He looked all around, and at last he found sleeping Princess Aurora.

'You truly are beautiful,' he told her. 'Would you mind if I kissed you?'

Of course, Princess Aurora couldn't answer.

'I will only kiss your hand,' said Prince Florimond. He gently lifted her hand, and he kissed it.

And Princess Aurora woke.
'Hello!' said Aurora, rubbing her eyes. 'Who are you?'

As Aurora and Florimond talked, everyone in the palace awoke. The fires came to life. Water in the fountain flowed. The cooks got cooking. Gardeners picked flowers. Dogs barked. The King and Queen hurried to find their daughter.

'This is Prince Florimond,' Princess Aurora told them. 'He woke us all up.'

'In that case he must stay for dinner!' said the King.

Prince Florimond didn't just stay for dinner. He stayed for days and weeks. They all liked him very much. Princess Aurora liked him the best of all. It wasn't long before she decided to marry him.

They had the grandest of weddings. The King wrote the invitations. How many fairies do you think he invited to the wedding party?

Eight! The nasty fairy was given the best of everything at the party. That made her happy, and almost nice. So she gave Aurora and Florimond a wonderful wedding present ... if you like that sort of thing!